The Point Street Garden

by Rachel Russ

illustrated by Adam Walker-Parker

Anya was visiting her nan. Nan had not been living in her flat for long.

Anya and Nan had a drink.

“Do you miss your garden?” asked Anya.

“Yes, but I like this flat,” said Nan.

Just then, a booklet dropped from the letterbox.

"Oh!" said Anya. "There will be a garden for the flats. They need gardeners to help!"

The next morning, they went to see the garden.

"I am Marvin," said a man. "Have you come to help?"

"Yes," said Anya. "My nan loves gardening."

Nan grabbed a trowel. She showed Anya how to ...

dig up the weeds ...

sow their seeds ...

keep their seeds moist.

They had fun gardening. Nan met lots of people from the flats.

Anya went to Nan's flat at the weekends.
She wanted to help with the garden.

On one visit, Anya spotted green shoots.

“We must nurture them,” said Nan.
“Seedlings need sun and water.”

Soon the garden was full of bright blooms. There were rows of radishes and beetroots.

“We can have a summer picnic,” said Marvin.
“We should have it in the garden.”

The next weekend, they all had their picnic.

"Now you have a garden, Nan," said Anya.

"There are lots of gardeners, too!"
added Nan.

Grow a Seedling!

1. Put soil in a pot.

2. Drop a seed in.

3. Put soil on top.

4. It will need sun and water.

5. See the seedling grow!

Encourage students to read the instructions about how to grow a seedling.